PROCESSION OF COACHES FROM ST PAUL'S

The 1902 State landau: The Bride and Bridegroom

Queen Alexandra's State Coach: Prince Edward, India Hicks, Catherine Cameron and Sarah Jane Gaselee

The Glass Coach: Lady Sarah Armstrong-Jones, Lord Nicholas Windsor, Clementine Hambro and Edward van Cutsem

In an open semi-state landau: the Queen and Lord Spencer

In a State landau: the Duke of Edinburgh and the Hon Mrs Shand Kydd

In a State landau: the Queen Mother and Prince Andrew

In a State landau: Princess Anne, Capt. Mark Phillips, Princess Margaret and Viscount Linley

In a State landau: Princess Alice, the Duke of Gloucester, the Duchess of Gloucester and the Earl of Ulster

In a State landau: the Duke of Kent, the Duchess of Kent, the Earl of St Andrews and Lady Helen Windsor

In a State landau: Prince Michael of Kent, Princess Michael of Kent, the Duchess of Grafton and the Earl of Westmorland

In a State landau: Princess Alexandra, Angus Ogilvy, James Ogilvy and Marina Ogilvy

Royal Wedding

by AUDREY DALY

Photographs by JOHN SCOTT

Ladybird Books Loughborough

The Lord Chamberlain is Commanded by
The Queen and The Duke of Edinburgh to invite

....

to the Marriage of
His Royal Highness The Prince of Wales
with
The Lady Diana Spencer
in St. Paul's Cathedral
on Wednesday, 29th July, 1981 at 11.00 a.m.

An answer is requested to the Lord Chamberlain,
St. James's Palace, London, S.W.1.

Dress: Uniform, Morning Dress
or Lounge Suit.

On the eve of the wedding, a magnificent Grand Concert and Firework Display was given in Hyde Park, in aid of the International Year of the Disabled, of which Prince Charles is President.

Prince Charles lit the first of a series of beacons which carried the news of his forthcoming marriage, to the furthest parts of the United Kingdom in under an hour.

A huge firework palace had been built, and special firework effects such as the crests and badges of the regiments of which the Prince of Wales is Colonel in Chief exploded into the night sky, ending with an enormous Catherine-wheel thirty-five feet across.

Over half a million people crowded into Hyde Park to watch the display and to enjoy the music of massed bands and choirs.

When it was over, many people spent the rest of the night along the royal route, instead of going home.

Eight o'clock in the morning — and London was already full of smiling faces. Even those who had been sleeping on the pavements, to be sure of a good place at the front of the waiting crowds, looked pleased and happy. It was Wednesday 29th July 1981 — declared by Royal Proclamation a public holiday for the wedding of the heir to the throne, Prince Charles, and his chosen bride Lady Diana Spencer.

Invitations to over two thousand six hundred people were sent out several weeks before the great day. At this moment, guests all over London were getting ready to attend the ceremony in St Paul's Cathedral.

Every street was bright with banners and decorations, and all the flagpoles — forty-two of them on the royal route — carried a crown, symbol of royalty. Lamp posts wore a dainty floral collar in the form of flower baskets with pink, purple and silver flowers, specially grown by the Royal Parks Department.

Everything was freshly painted, clean and new, ready for the royal progress. The dustcarts kept going the rounds to cheers from the crowd.

In some places the crowd was more than twenty deep — not just Londoners, but people from all over the world, all intent on enjoying the celebrations. Fruit stalls, hot dog stands, and tea and coffee stalls did a roaring business. Flags were everywhere, and there were some very strange sights to be seen — a wedding cake hat, red, white and blue hair — and even red, white and blue faces.

It was a warm sunny morning, and thousands of people, ranging from babes in arms to people over eighty, were just wandering around the streets, waiting for the start of the great occasion.

Quite early in the day, the regiments of footguards marched to their places on the processional route providing a foretaste of the spectacle to come for those already lining the route.

Many creative
hours must have
been spent in
making the
hundreds of
banners to be seen
amongst the crowd.
Some had amusing
captions such as
"Long live rock and
royal", and the one
featured here.

The
Wedding
Route

Buckingham Palace

Admiralty Arch

Queen Victoria Memorial

THE MALL

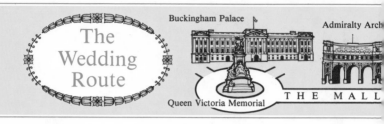

Over two thousand policemen were on duty to make sure the day stayed a happy one. There were policemen only a hand's touch apart in front, and at the back, of the crowd. Every room in every building along the procession route had been checked each day over the previous fortnight, and every

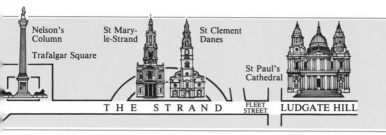

Nelson's Column

Trafalgar Square

St Mary-le-Strand

St Clement Danes

St Paul's Cathedral

THE STRAND FLEET STREET LUDGATE HILL

member of every party using those rooms had been vetted by the police.

On the wedding day itself, all the checking was done one last time, and even St Paul's Cathedral was examined by policemen with dogs trained to sniff out explosives. Helicopters flew overhead, and there were police watching from rooftops and windows along the two mile route. An armed policeman, disguised as a footman, travelled on the Queen's coach, and one on the Prince of Wales' coach both before and after the ceremony. This was a day on which nothing must go wrong.

After the wedding, the bride and groom travelled together, and their coach was escorted by the Household Cavalry.

A captain in the Household Cavalry

Mounted policeman in ceremonial dress

11

Right up to the morning of the wedding, presents were arriving for the happy couple. Prince Charles' great personal popularity led to his receiving one or two rather strange gifts. One, for example, was a brass paperweight from Dartmoor Prison — in the symbolic shape of a ball and chain!

From 9.30 onwards, a steady stream of cars brought guests from far and wide to the cathedral, for the congregation had to be seated by ten o'clock. There were many official guests from abroad. Both families, as with all weddings were well represented, but there were also many personal friends of the bride and bridegroom, amongst them celebrities from the world of show business, the designers of the bridal gown, Lady Diana's hairdresser, her three ex-flatmates and Miss Jean Lowe, headmistress of the bride's first school.

In the Queen's Procession were Princess Anne with her husband and Princess Margaret with her son, Viscount Linley. Princess Margaret wore a coral silk outfit and Princess Anne wore a striking white and yellow dress in heavy printed silk with an eye-catching hat.

(top right)
Travelling with Princess Alice, Duchess of Gloucester were the Duke and Duchess of Gloucester and their son the Earl of Ulster

(bottom right)
The Duke and Duchess of Kent rode in the fifth carriage with their children, the Earl of St Andrews and Lady Helen Windsor

As the Queen and Prince Philip rode to the
cathedral in the semi state landau, both of them
looked relaxed and happy.

The Queen wore a pale aquamarine silk dress and jacket, with matching hat and purse, and Prince Philip wore the uniform of Admiral of the Fleet.

A view of the high altar with the choirs and clergy ready for their part in the service

On arrival at the west door, the Queen and Prince Philip were greeted by the clergy who were to officiate at the marriage ceremony. The Lord Mayor bearing aloft the pearl sword, led the Queen and Prince Philip down the long aisle to their seats under the dome.

The organist played a Rondeau by Henry Purcell during the Queen's procession.

Prince Charles and his supporter
Prince Andrew, on their way to St Paul's

As the famous Glass Coach came out of the gates of Clarence House the world had its first glimpse of the twenty year old bride wearing a dress designed by Welsh designers David and Elizabeth Emanuel, and made from pure silk spun in Suffolk.

It was her last journey as Lady Diana Spencer, escorted by a combined escort of Royal Military (Mounted) Police and Metropolitan Police (Mounted Branch).

As the bride's procession moved down the aisle the vast congregation caught their first glimpse of the ivory silk taffeta wedding dress with its twenty five foot long train. Behind her were the five bridesmaids also in ivory satin, with gold sashes and lemon satin slippers. They carried very pretty flower baskets.

Chief bridesmaid was Lady Sarah Armstrong-Jones, aged 17, daughter of Princess Margaret and Lord Snowdon. The youngest — aged 5 — was Clementine Hambro, who is a pupil at the Young England Kindergarten where Lady Diana used to teach. She is a great grand-daughter of Sir Winston Churchill.

The other three bridesmaids were India Hicks, aged 14, daughter of Mr David and Lady Pamela Hicks, Catherine Cameron, aged 6, daughter of Donald Cameron of Lochiel and Lady Cecil Cameron, and Sarah Jane Gaselee, aged 10, daughter of Mr and Mrs Nick Gaselee (Mr Gaselee trains race horses for Prince Charles).

The two pages were eleven year old Lord Nicholas Windsor, and eight year old Edward van Cutsem, both of whom are godsons of Prince Charles. They wore naval uniforms of the time of 1863.

*The congregation sang ''Christ is made the sure foundation'',
the first hymn*

Then came the time
honoured and familiar
ritual of the marriage
ceremony, watched by a
world-wide television
audience of seven
hundred and fifty
million, and relayed by
loudspeaker to the
crowds outside the
Cathedral.

The Archbishop of
Canterbury, Dr Robert
Runcie, conducted the
service assisted by the
Very Reverend Alan
Webster, Dean of St
Paul's. In the form of
service chosen, the word
"obey" was not part of
the bride's vows. At the
appropriate moment,
Prince Andrew, who was
acting as Prince Charles'
principal supporter, (by
tradition, there was no
best man) handed him
the wedding ring. It was
made of Welsh gold.

*The Queen Mother watched
the young couple
with affection and
obvious emotion*

The gold was from the same nugget from which the wedding rings of the Queen and Queen Mother, as well as those of Princess Margaret and Princess Anne, were made.

Although both bride and groom appeared to be enjoying the occasion, their nervousness showed when they each made a small mistake in their responses.

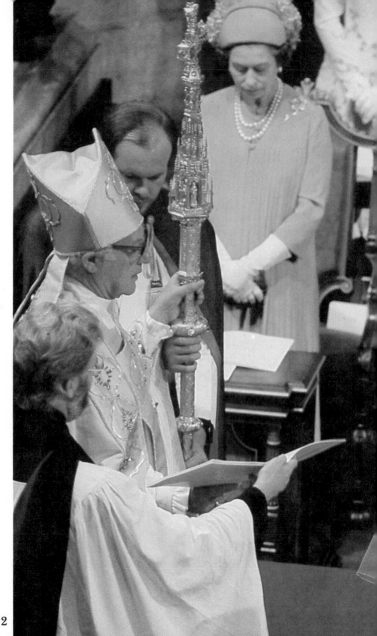

The ceremony over, the Archbishop of Canterbury pronounced the Blessing, and the congregation sang the National Anthem. Then the Princess of Wales went to the vestry with her new husband to sign her maiden name for the last time.

It was witnessed by Her Majesty the Queen and Prince Philip, amongst others.

While the register was being signed, an aria from Handel's *Samson* was sung by the world famous soprano from New Zealand, Kiri Te Kanawa, and the Bach Choir.

Then the bride and bridegroom made their way down the aisle, to a Fanfare of trumpets played by the State Trumpeters, conducted by Major Anthony Richards.

The Archbishop pronounced the Blessing

As the trumpet fanfare sounded within the
cathedral, the crowds grew quiet with expectancy.
Then came the bold notes of the famous Elgar
march, *Pomp and Circumstance*, as the Prince and
Princess made their way slowly down the aisle.

Outside, every eye focussed on the West Door —
including over seven hundred and fifty *million*
people all over the world, who watched it live on
television — the biggest audience ever known.

Then out they came, to a cheer that went on and
on and on — for a prince who has earned his
popularity the hard way, and his brand new wife,
whose charm and naturalness have delighted the
British public.

And as Prince Charles handed his Princess into
their carriage, the bells began to peal. All over the
country, other bells joined in, a joyful sound of
celebration.

Leaving St Paul's after the ceremony

*The Prince of Wales and his new Princess of Wales were obviously
thrilled and delighted by the large, enthusiastic, happy crowd*

In the wake of the bridal coach, Prince Edward and three of the bridesmaids — India Hicks, Sarah Jane Gaselee and Catherine Cameron — returned to Buckingham Palace in Queen Alexandra's State Coach (built in 1865).

The Glass Coach returned to the Palace carrying the other two bridesmaids and the two pages — Lady Sarah Armstrong-Jones, Lord Nicholas Windsor, Clementine Hambro and Edward van Cutsem.

On the way back to Buckingham Palace, the Queen travelled in the first coach with Prince Charles' new father-in-law, Earl Spencer. The Duke of Edinburgh was in the second coach with Mrs Shand Kydd, now mother-in-law to Prince Charles.

Charles and Diana appeared on the balcony
repeatedly in response to demands from the enthusiastic
crowds massed below. The youngest page, Edward van

Cutsem (seen left), remained on the balcony by himself, to the amusement of the crowd. Little Clemmie Hambro was less fascinated!

This photograph of the royal couple on the balcony was flashed to thousands of newspapers all over the world — delighting millions as it put the final seal on this fairy tale romance.

This traditional wedding photograph of bride and groom, supporters and bridesmaids will undoubtedly feature in the family albums of all involved. The group consists of, from left to right: Edward van Cutsem; seated in front, Catherine Cameron; and above her, Lord Nicholas Windsor. On his left, India Hicks, and in front of her, Sarah Jane Gaselee. On Prince Charles' right stands Prince Edward, and on the Princess's left, Prince Andrew. On the far right, Lady Sarah Armstrong-Jones; and seated, Clementine Hambro.

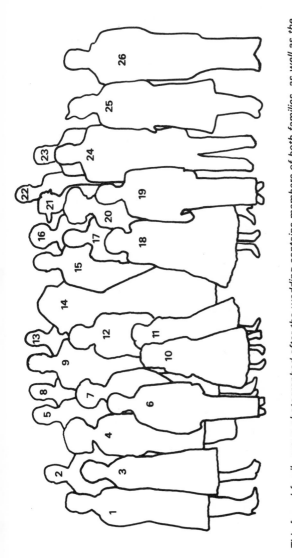

This formal family group photographed after the wedding contains members of both families, as well as the bridesmaids and pages. 1, Princess Anne; 2, Capt. Mark Phillips; 3, Princess Margaret; 4, Queen Elizabeth, the Queen Mother; 5, Prince Andrew; 6, Edward van Cutsem; 7, Her Majesty the Queen; 8, Viscount Linley; 9, Prince Philip; 10, Clementine Hambro; 11, Catherine Cameron; 12, India Hicks; 13, Prince Edward; 14, The Princess of Wales; 15, The Prince of Wales; 16, Ruth, Lady Fermoy; 17, Lady Sarah Armstrong-Jones; 18, Sarah Jane Gaselee; 19, Lord Nicholas Windsor; 20, Mrs Shand Kydd; 21, Lady Jane Fellowes; 22, Viscount Althorp; 23, Mr Robert Fellowes; 24, 8th Earl Spencer; 25, Lady Sarah McCorquodale; 26, Mr Neil McCorquodale

47

Then it was time for the wedding cake! Prince Charles and his new Princess of Wales made the traditional first cut. This cake — five feet tall with five tiers — was made by the Royal Naval Cookery School at Chatham with every raisin hand-picked by Chief Petty Officer David Avery and his assistants — it took half an hour to crack all the eggs that were needed! Several designs for the icing were drawn by the Naval Technical Drawing Department for approval by the bride. The cake was made in March to give time for the flavour to improve, and four weeks was allowed for the icing. No doubt, true to tradition, the top tier will be put away for the christening! Each of the five tiers was decorated

with pastel-tinted plaques showing places and motifs connected with the couple.

There were fifteen other very beautifully decorated cakes on show as well, which had been made by people with some connection either with the Queen or the Prince and Princess.

The Princess's bouquet was white and gold stephanotis, gardenias, orchids, lily of the valley and yellow Earl Mountbatten roses. It also contained the traditional sprig of myrtle, symbol of love, and veronica taken from bushes grown from cuttings from Queen Victoria's bouquet. The bouquet was later placed on the Tomb of the Unknown Soldier

True to tradition, the Prince and Princess left before the party was over. The Princess wore a coral pink dress and a tricorne hat with ostrich feathers. She had a happy smile for the crowd which had waited so patiently throughout the wedding breakfast. Prince Charles, at her side, looked equally happy in spite of the strain of a long day.

Their carriage was decorated with twenty blue and silver balloons and a "Just Married" placard (the work of Princes Andrew and Edward). They went to Waterloo Station, where they left by train for Romsey in Hampshire. There they stayed a few days at Broadlands, the home of the late Earl Mountbatten of Burma.

Broadlands has always been a favourite of the royal family — the Queen and the Duke of Edinburgh spent part of *their* honeymoon there in 1947.

The Prince and Princess later cruised in the Mediterranean, on the royal yacht *Britannia*.

Broadlands, where the Prince and Princess of Wales spent the first part of their honeymoon